# THE AMERICAN EAGLE

## AMERICAN SYMBOLS

Lynda Sorensen

The Rourke Book Company, Inc.
Vero Beach, Florida 32964

PHOTO CREDITS
All photos © Lynn M. Stone except page 4, © James P. Rowan
and page 17, courtesy of U.S. State Department

ACKNOWLEDGMENTS
The author thanks the Brookfield Zoo for its cooperation in the
preparation of this book.

**Library of Congress Cataloging-in-Publication Data**

Sorensen, Lynda, 1953–
    American Eagle / by Lynda Sorensen
        p.  cm. — (American symbols)
    Includes index.
    ISBN 1-55916-045-4
    1. United States—Seal—Juvenile literature. 2. Bald Eagle—
Juvenile literature. 3. Signs and symbols—United States—Juvenile
literature.
[1. United States—Seal. 2. Bald Eagle.  3. Eagles  4. Signs and
symbols.]
I. Title  II. Series.
CD5610.S67 1994
929.8'2—dc20                                  94–7051
                                                CIP
Printed in the USA                              AC

# TABLE OF CONTENTS

# THE AMERICAN EAGLE

The bald eagle became a **symbol** of the United States shortly after the nation was founded.

A symbol stands for something other than itself. America chose the bald eagle as a symbol because it stood for freedom and strength.

The bald eagle, often called "the American eagle," appears on the Great Seal of the United States. Its likeness also appears on some coins, on paper money and on many other objects.

*American eagle perched on the old Custom House at Salem Maritime National Historic Site*

# EAGLE OR TURKEY?

Benjamin Franklin was an important figure in founding the new United States in the late 1700's. It seems that Mr. Franklin wanted the wild turkey to be America's national symbol.

Mr. Franklin believed the tasty turkey was a more "noble" bird than the bald eagle. The bald eagle, he said, was not a proud bird. It fed on **carrion**—dead animals.

Mr. Franklin drew little support. Lawmakers were more impressed by the bald eagle. The United States Congress selected the bald eagle as a national symbol on June 20, 1782.

*Benjamin Franklin didn't approve of a national symbol that sometimes fed on carrion*

## A COWARD IT'S NOT

Mr. Franklin thought the bald eagle was cowardly. *He* was never dive-bombed by an eagle.

Truth is, a bald eagle in defense of its nest can be quite dangerous. Now and then it will make a swooping attack to drive a person away.

Mr. Franklin should have visited the bold bald eagles in the Aleutian Islands of Alaska. He might have changed his opinion of bald eagles.

*Talons down, a bald eagle swoops toward a hiker who approached too close to the eagle's nest in Alaska's Aleutian Islands*

# THE NOBLE EAGLE

The bald eagle was a wise choice as America's national bird. It is a handsome, fierce-looking bird of prey. It lives almost entirely in North America. At one time or another it can be found in every state.

The bald eagle is one of the world's largest and most powerful hunting birds. It often kills live prey with its sharp claws, called **talons**. Its wingspread—the distance from the tip of one wing to another—can reach eight feet.

*A deadly hunter, the bald eagle strikes with amazing speed and strength*

*Ben Franklin's choice for a national bird would have been a turkey*

*The bald eagle spends the first four or five years of its life without its white crown and tail feathers*

## EAGLES EVERYWHERE

The bald eagle turns up every time someone passes a dollar bill, a quarter, a half dollar or a silver dollar. An image of the eagle also appears on old American gold coins called "eagles."

More than 25 different American stamps have shown bald eagles. Metal eagles perch on flagpoles and government buildings. The Boy Scouts' highest rank is Eagle Scout.

Several states show a bald eagle on their official state seals.

*The bald eagle was golden on American coins called "eagles"*

# THE EAGLE ON THE GREAT SEAL

The Great Seal of the United States is the nation's official stamp. It appears on important papers of the United States Government. The seal is also displayed at government meetings.

The bald eagle is at the center of the Great Seal. The eagle holds an olive branch in the talons of one foot. The olive branch symbolizes peace. The other foot holds arrows, standing for strength.

*The bald eagle is the centerpiece of America's Great Seal*

# THE AMERICAN EAGLE IN TROUBLE

The bald eagle on the nation's Great Seal has remained more or less the same. That cannot be said for the real bald eagle.

For many years the great, white-headed birds were shot and their nest trees were often chopped down. Alaska paid a **bounty**, or payment, to people who killed bald eagles! More than 100,000 bald eagles were turned in for bounties between 1917 and 1952. Some Alaskans said eagles were killing too many salmon and farm-raised Arctic foxes.

By 1960 the national bird was finally protected by law throughout the United States.

*For 35 years the Territory of Alaska paid*
*bounties for dead bald eagles*

# SAVING THE NATIONAL SYMBOL

In the 1960's bald eagles faced a new problem in the lower 48 states. The numbers of bald eagles dropped rapidly.

The problem was a chemical known as DDT. DDT was used to kill insects, but it washed into streams, rivers and oceans. Fish swallowed some of it, and eagles ate the poisoned fish. The effect of the poison caused eagle eggs to break.

The use of DDT in the United States was stopped in the early 1970's. The bald eagle's future began to brighten.

*The bald eagle's future soared with new laws that were made to protect the national symbol*

# THE SYMBOL ON THE WING

The times when people freely shot bald eagles are over. It is a crime to harm a bald eagle.

Most Americans treat the eagle with respect. They are thrilled to see a bald eagle.

The best news is that the bald eagle is returning to many of its old hangouts. More people will be able to see America's national bird on the wing.

## Glossary

**bounty** (BOUN tee) — a payment for the killing of certain animals; a reward offered by the government

**carrion** (KARE ee un) — dead animals

**symbol** (SIM bull) — something which stands for something else, as a flag stands for a country

**talon** (TAH lun) — the claws on the feet of birds of prey, such as eagles

# INDEX